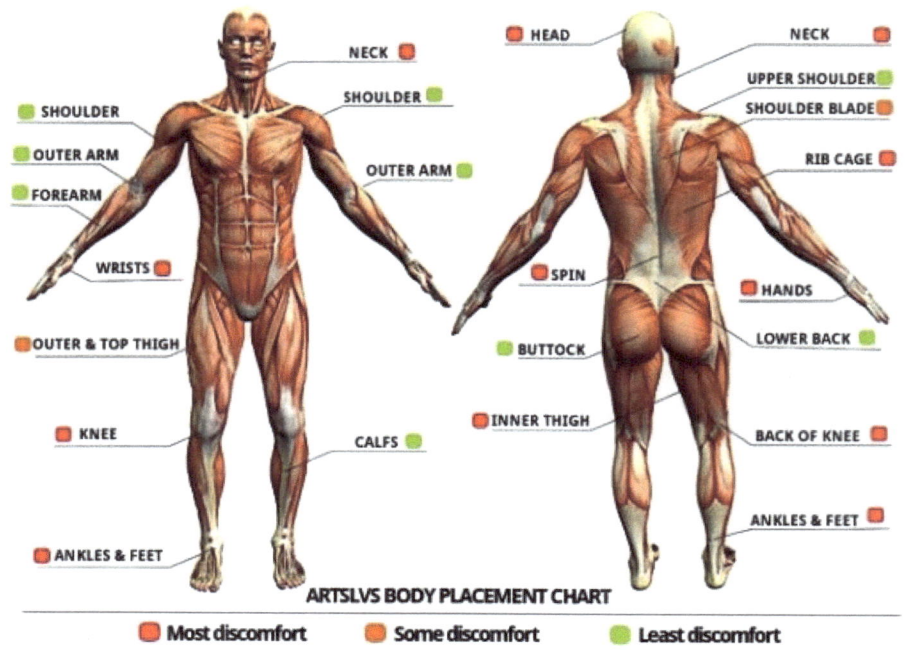

Getting a tattoo requires a lot of preparation. I should know –I am a professional artist and have documented the process to tell the world a little bit more about what goes into getting inked, from choosing a design \

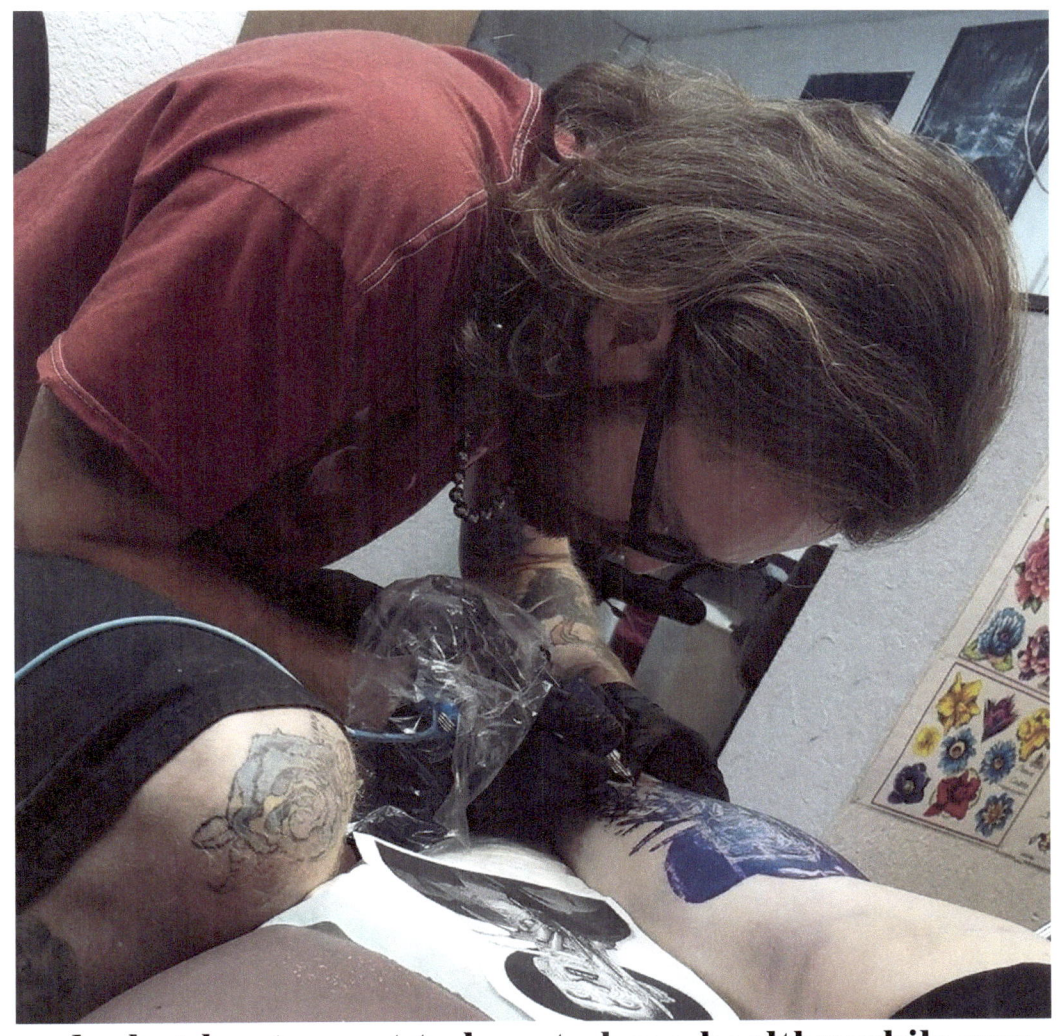

and what hurts most to how to keep healthy while you heal.

Decide what you want and where you want to put it.

you should feel confident that your tattoo is the right thing for you. You can seek inspiration from photographs, aesthetics that strike you, or your own imagination.

Along with knowing what you want, you should also have an idea of where and how big you want your tattoo to be before you move much further on with the process.

For me, the process of settling on a tattoo has lasted between a couple of months and several years.

Consider the following when choosing where to get tattooed:

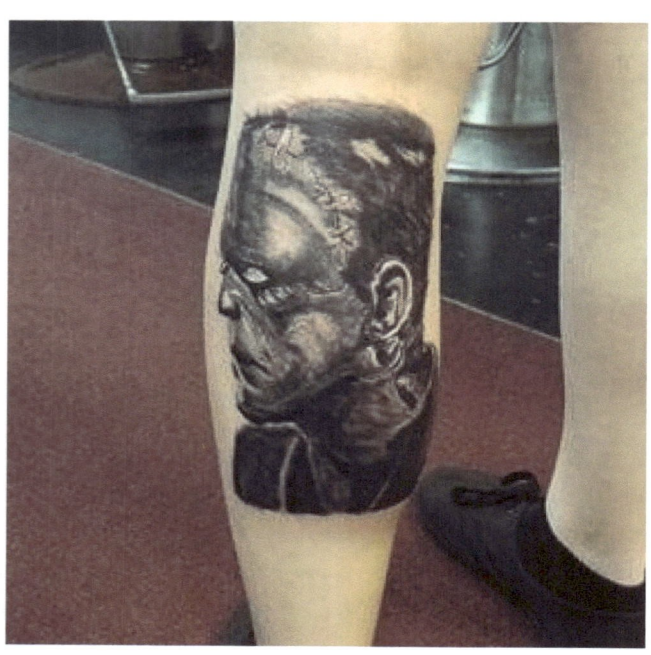

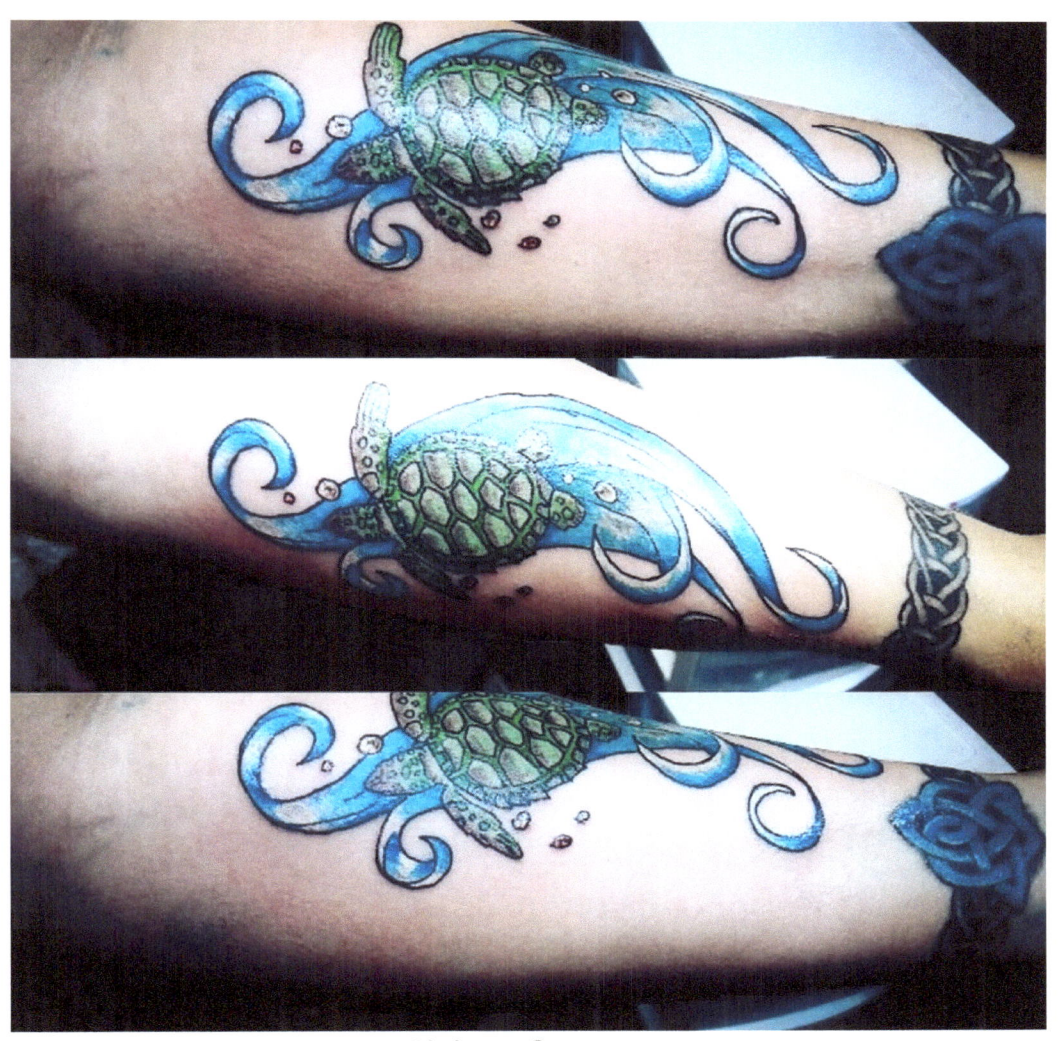

Do you have any conditions?

if you have a pre-existing skin condition, you should consult a doctor in advance of your tattoo. He said it's best not to have a tattoo done over a mole. "The tattoo ink will not cause any changes to the mole. "However, the ink may disguise changes in the size, shape, or colour of the mole in the future, making it difficult to diagnose early signs of skin cancer." tattooing over scars. This can be done, "given the scar isn't too raised "It is best to not work over the scar until it is at least a couple of years old and has stopped changing its form."

You should also discuss any other significant health concerns with a doctor and your tattoo artist. Drew street Tattoo in Florida requires that you inform the studio in advance if you suffer from heart disease, eczema, impetigo, allergic reactions to medical soap, adhesive plasters, disinfectant, haemmorhaging, fainting, epilepsy, or blood-borne viruses. You should not get a tattoo while pregnant or breastfeeding.

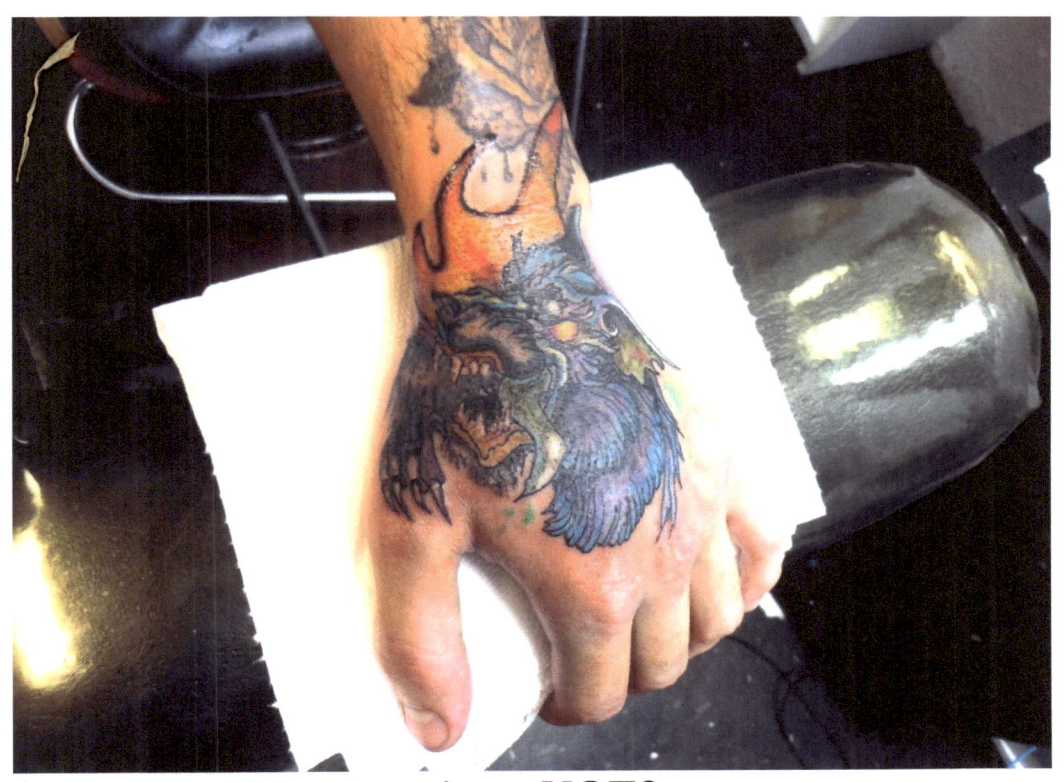

Are you sensitive to pain or NOT?

If you're SCARED about pain, you should be careful when planning the size and location of your tattoo. I have a fairly low pain tolerance, and still found my first two tattoos to be virtually painless, but my most recent experience taught me that the area around the inside of my elbow is extremely sensitive. Check out a pain chart for some basic information on areas you might want to avoid.

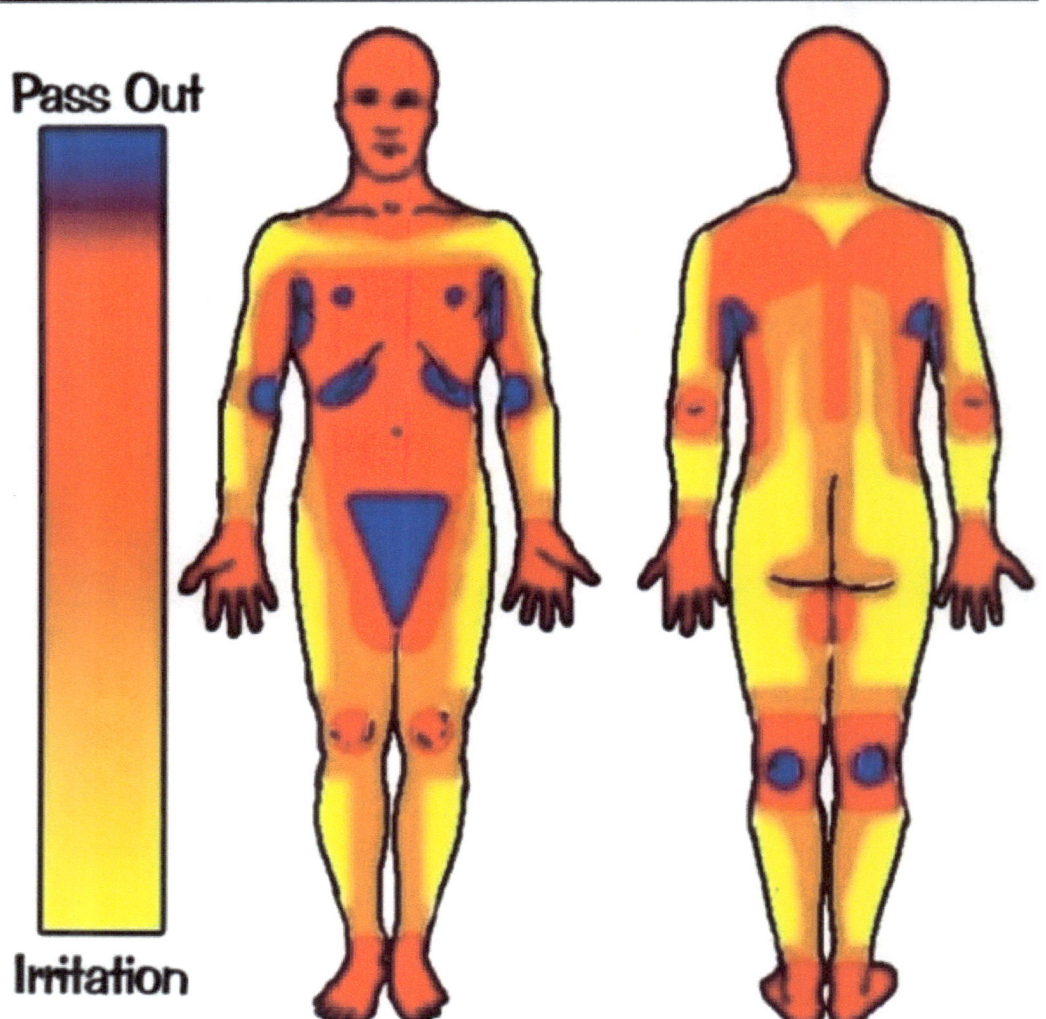

Can you display tattoos at work?

If you're working, make sure you know your employer's stance on tattoos. If they need to be covered, you'll need to take into account how easy that will be for you to do.

"Although it has become much more accepted in recent years, a decision to tattoo the neck, hands or face should not be taken lightly,"

Communicate your ideas to your artist.

Once you've decided on a tattoo and an artist, it's essential to establish an open communication with your artist so that you feel comfortable throughout the process. A good rapport and sense of trust with your artist will help you feel confident during the tattooing process.

To get this going, you should arrange a consultation before your tattoo so you can discuss your ideas with your artist, and so you can get an idea of what it will cost and what the process will be like. If you can be in touch via email before your consultation, you can take the opportunity to put your thoughts and ideas in writing, and send along some visual inspiration to give your artist a sense of what you're going for.

years of experience and artistic intuition have made Drew street tattoo the kind of shop that just gets it. We are quick to understand many ideas and make adjustments based on your thoughts. "There is a personal way to draw anything," is the shops moto, and we stand by it–

One of the most wonderful aspects of getting a tattoo is the collaboration between your ideas and those of your artist. "having the freedom to be creative every day and the challenge of translating peoples ideas onto skin" is one of the most fulfilling parts for us as well.

It's incredibly important to keep your mind open to your artist's ideas and see what they can bring to the table when it comes to style and personalisation.

Arrange your appointment.

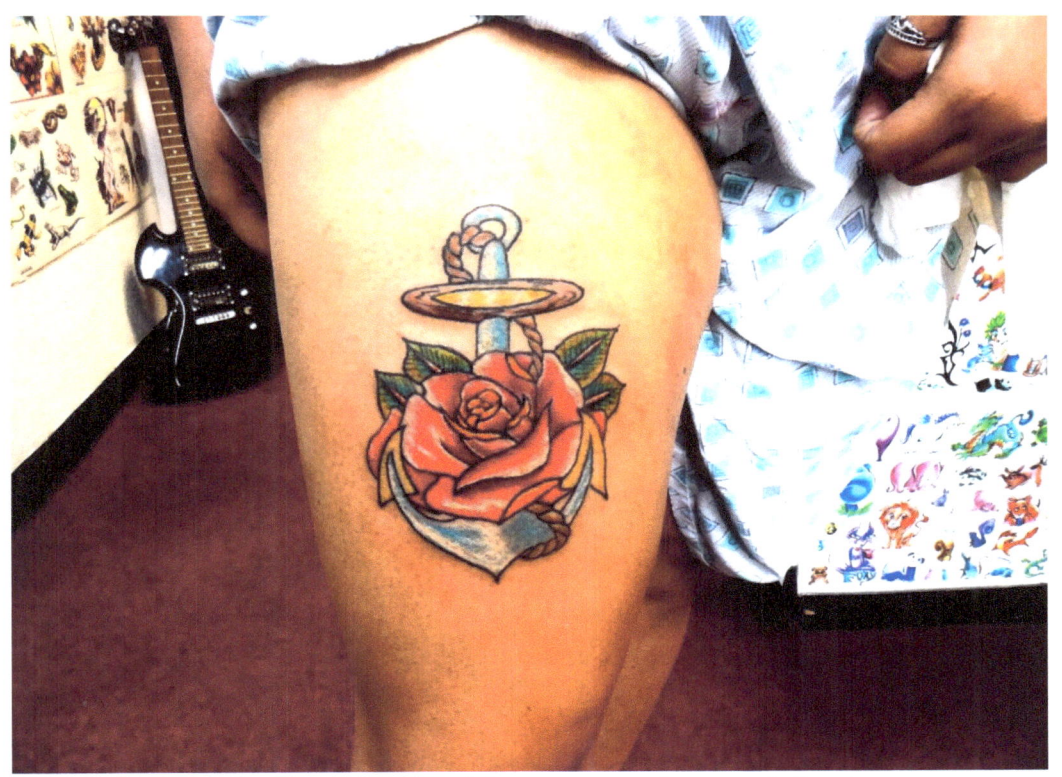

Once you've had a chat with your artist and feel comfortable placing your skin in their hands, you'll need to set up an appointment for your tattoo. Some shops may be able to do it on the day, while others may require several weeks' notice – it's good to check on your artist's policy.

Most tattoo studios require a deposit, so come to your consultation prepared to put down some cash, and be aware of the refund policy. In my case, the deposit came to about one-third of the total cost of my tattoo.

You should try to get a price quote so that you can know the budget for your final appointment. Your artist may tell you it will depend on the final size and time, in which case you should ask what the cap on the price will be so you can put aside a general figure for the appointment.

Get health and safety concerns in order.

When you arrive on the day of your tattoo appointment, you'll be asked to sign a health and safety waiver. You'll need to provide some basic information to make sure you're in good health and to release the shop from responsibility for any liabilities caused by the tattoo. If you've done your safety research and confirmed that your studio meets health and safety standards according to your local council, as well as making sure you feel physically comfortable in the shop, this is no problem.

My copy of the waiver also had my care instructions on the back – it's best to hang on to those!

Finalise the design.

Going over the final design is a hugely important step on the day of your tattoo. When I arrived, Mo had already drafted up several versions of the design we discussed so that we could settle on what to move forward with.

We considered a couple of options we'd previously discussed – including the idea of putting my favourite (and spirit) animal, a turtle, at the base of the parachute. While we had both liked the idea at the consultation, it was clear once the drawings were done that the size I wanted wouldn't allow for proper detail to make the turtle look as delicate as I imagined, so I was happy to let that go in lieu of the simpler image of a heart. Once we settled on a size that I felt comfortable with, Mo was off to the drawing table to finalise my tattoo design.

Transfer the tattoo stencil.

After the design is set, it's time to settle into the chair, but before the needles come out, most studios allow you to "try on" your tattoo using a stencil. This also serves as the guide during the actual tattooing process. Some artists draw freehand, like I do at the shop but it's best to be very careful with that kind of approach it can get expensive.

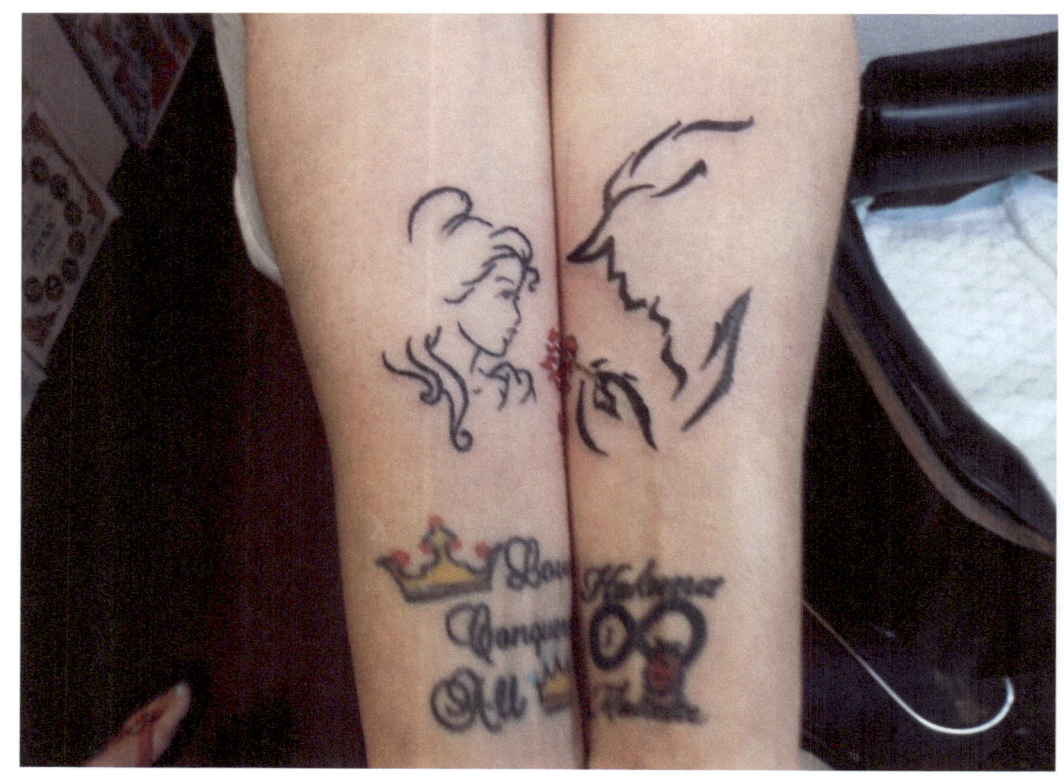

Once you're ready, it's outline time.

!

The outline can take 15min to 100 hours some say it feels, like a scratch

There's a lot more ink involved than actually goes into your skin, which leads to a bit of mess and smear over the top. It may cause the lines of your tattoo to look distorted at first, but in my experience that's fairly normal. Once starting the tattoo you should trust your artist.

If you're getting a tattoo in an area you can easily see, you should definitely watch the process, even if you're squeamish. It's great to keep an eye on things so that you're comfortable with the progress, but more importantly, it's quite mesmerizing to watch, and the experience of seeing it happen weaves itself into your lasting memory of the tattoo.

Shading is the fun part.

To be completely honest, this part is the BEST. You'll notice more blood than you did during the outlining process, but this is normal – a large area of skin is being tattooed at once in this case, so it's to be expected.

The best advice I can give here is try to stay still and breathe; so despite some discomfort, it IS quite manageable. Larger and more sensitive areas may take longer and be more painful depending on you, so consult your artist and refer back to a pain chart if you're concerned.

Colour is the final touch.

When you're planning a tattoo with your artist, you should discuss how different shades will look on your skin, as well as how different styles of colouring might look with the rest of your tattoo.

The process for colour isn't any different than using black ink; again

Keep your tattoo covered for the first several hours.

.

You won't need to rewrap the area after you've removed your inital dressing, but with the tattoo so fresh, it's best to avoid letting it come in contact with fibres or other irritants and keep it washed regularly.

Wash and moisturise regularly, but not excessively.

In the weeks that follow, your tattoo will go through several stages of healing, and it's important to give it excellent care. The Family Business suggests gently washing it three times daily with a mild soap such as Dial and applying a moisturising cream several times a day. You should avoid anything with fragrance – The Family Business's aftercare sheet suggests its in-house cream, or

Bepanthen or Acriflex as an alternative. Drew street Tattoo and Piercing also recommends Dial soap and medical grade A&D + E ointment

You should always wash your hands before moisturizing, and only use enough cream to "keep it slightly moist", The Family Business advises. I find it best to apply cream when I can sit still for 15–20 minutes while it dries, as Bepanthen is a bit greasy and can smear your clothes or get things stuck to it if you're moving the tattooed area about.

Be aware of what you expose a healing tattoo to.

While you should be keeping your tattoo clean, you should avoid over soaking it soaking your tattoo in the bath or exposing it to direct sunlight can be very harmful during the healing process". So be advised that you should wait to shave the area until the tattoo is fully healed. "Follow the aftercare instructions given to you by your artist and your tattoo will heal beautifully,"

When it comes to working out, you don't need to disrupt your whole routine, but maybe take things down a notch while you heal. "As long as you don't over-sweat, you can do some light exercise,".

Follow your tattooist's instructions when it comes to aftercare.

OTHER THINGS YOU NEED TO KNOW!

If you want to bring a friend, go for it, but there's no need to roll in with a massive posse like you're on your death bed.

This is one of those things that many people feel intimidated to do alone, so bringing someone with is normal. However, I was told that it becomes an issue when people legitimately bring a basketball roster's worth of people in their entourage, especially when it's a group of teenagers who interact on the highest of volumes while horsing around and touching things the entire time. A friend or two in attendance makes sense, but 5+ are excessive for anything but Applebee's happy hour or your funeral.

2. You're not going to be able to get an entire, massive piece on your back or full arm sleeve in a half hour.

Apparently it isn't uncommon for people to walk in tattoo shops without making an appointment and expect to be able, not only to get a large tattoo, but to have it completed absurdly hastily. Larger works typically require multiple sessions that are scheduled out over time.

3. You've absolutely got to control any fidgety, squirmy, jerky, convulsiveness.

If your pain tolerance won't allow you to remain still throughout the process, you may not be tattoo-able. You're putting the aesthetics of your permanent body art at risk and one artist siad, *"There's no room for error on my part. When it comes to mistakes, even if it's your fault, it's my fault. The artist takes the fall for 100% of screw-ups."* The video below is a prime example of a person who can't help but scream and wriggle her way to annoying the artist, though it appears that she isn't necessarily trying to be obnoxious, she's just not capable of handling the pain.

4. Be prepared to spend some money.

Larger sized tattoos (at least quality ones) aren't cheap. Much like dining out, if you can't really afford it then you should just not do it. It'll cost you a little cash and there are shop minimums that some people are surprised by because, for some unexplainable reason, they anticipated spending $20 on multiple hours worth of extremely careful work. If you want a large piece it'll likely be charged by the hour, which can make it somewhat difficult for the artist to give a super accurate estimate. It's also alarming when a potential customer says things like, *I was hoping not to spend more than $50"* because then it's a safe bet that they also don't intend to tip.

5. Tattoo shops aren't yard sales or sketchy flea markets, prices aren't often negotiable.

To those wondering if they can talk down a tattoo shop's prices, that's the equivalent of going in a store and giving the cashier a pitch as to why they should give you your groceries for 40% less. As the last point said and was often reiterated to me — if your bank account can't, don't.

6. At least have some idea of what you want.

One person compared the levels of frustration felt when a customer asks *"Do you have any ideas for what I should get?"* to "waiting in line behind someone who has no idea what they want at Subway." All those potential sandwich toppings don't compare to the infinite tattoo possibilities. If you have even a ballpark idea of what you want it can be further discussed, brainstormed and drawn out — but requesting concepts out of thin air is a little absurd.

7. If you want something cliché, go for it.

While there are some artists who may act high-and-mighty, smug, and judgmental about your tattoo choice, they should be few and far between. It's not the artist's job to understand why you want something on your body, it's their job to execute it as you desire. Even if they can't grasp why you'd want a particular piece, every artist I spoke with said that they keep confusion to themselves and look at everything as an opportunity to make money and more importantly, a permanent decision being made by a client that deserves 100% effort.

8. Eat a meal in advance… also, bathe.

The food is so you don't get lightheaded and/or faint, the bath is because you'd be surprised how many grown adults disregard hygiene despite knowing that they'll be in close quarters, and perhaps even have parts of their funky body exposed. One artist said, *"I had a client who reeked so bad he smelled like he'd glow neon green in the dark. He was **that** rancid."*

9. "We're not roughneck jerks… Well, we're not ALL roughneck jerks."

This was reiterated by a few who reassured me that you shouldn't be hesitant to go into a shop because of unapproachable appearances.

10. Don't bring kids with no supervision.

You'll be occupied and if the children are going to run free touching things it's really an inconvenience for the shop employees. (This should really apply to all public places.)

11. "Seriously consider getting a significant other's name permanently inked on your body…"

"… and if you still want it, reconsider until you've talked yourself out of it." No judging, but they all said they've seen how much of a disaster it is for those who regret it.

12. Don't overestimate your knowledge because you watch a tattoo reality show.

Those shows are entertaining and whatnot, sure, but don't let them convince you you're some type of expert who can condescendingly talk down to an artist because you caught a couple episodes of *Ink Master* the other day.

13. Don't come in munching on greasy ass food

That's just outright nasty and rude

14. Tats tatted got deez tats dawg…

Don't come into the shop acting like this its just annoying lmao but, whatever floats your boat.

WARNING: contains the following; double negatives, personal opinions, random bullshit – you HAVE been warned.

10 Ways to Piss Off Your Tattoo Artist!

1. Price check

You want to know how much that new tattoo is going to cost and you don't just want a "ball park" – oh *hell* no. You want an *exact quote* to the penny. Otherwise how will you be able to bargain hunt by calling up 3 or 4 different shops for the "best price"? you might end up black listed because we artist all know each other and talk.

Reality Check: Unless you are getting a piece of flash or tiny ass little word tattoo it is very hard for an artist to give an exact price. The factors that will affect the cost of your tattoo include; complexity of design, color and shading of design, your ability to take it like a man/woman, the speed at which your artist works *etc.* Don't ask for an *exact price* especially on large pieces like sleeves and backs. It's an ongoing process and good work is NOT cheap – deal with it.

2. Expect Your Artist to Read Your Mind

So you have this awesome idea for a tattoo and you want it to be "really rad" or "sick" so you convey this important info to the artist who has agreed to draw a custom design for you. Sure you don't know the details or anything – that is the artists job! So you tell them something like, "I want a big-ass DRAGON all but like totally sick...you know" and your artist –HE– goes home and spends a week or hours drawing a beautiful detailed drawing of a DRAGON right out his mind. When he shows you the sketch you say "Oh man I don't like it. I want the DRAGON to be way gnarlier – you know what I mean to fit in my mind the way I want?"

Reality Check: Your artist does NOT "know what you mean" – you have to be specific. Tattoo artists are not mind readers – they are artists. And before you ask an artist to draw something custom make sure you are both on the same page AND they draw in the style you like. The above example is a true story. Not only did she waste his time on that original sketch he spent another 3 hours drawing a new one for the person just to walk out on the deal a week later.

3. Steal Your Tattoo Artists Work

So you found a killer artist to do a custom sketch for you. You hammered out all the details and he fuckin nailed it! But whoa hang on there – this guy charges like $150 an hour and the shop next to the laundromat has a sign posted out front that says they only charge $50 bucks an hour – what's a bro to do? Grab your kick ass custom sketch and go save some big time money dude!

Reality Check: In the land of dick moves this one is King. Don't do that shit...Just. Don't. And don't print images from online of a popular artists custom work and then ask someone else to copy it for you. Copying is lame and potentially illegal (some artists are now copyrighting their work). A truly reputable artist will be *at least* uncomfortable and most likely unwilling to copy another artists custom design anyway

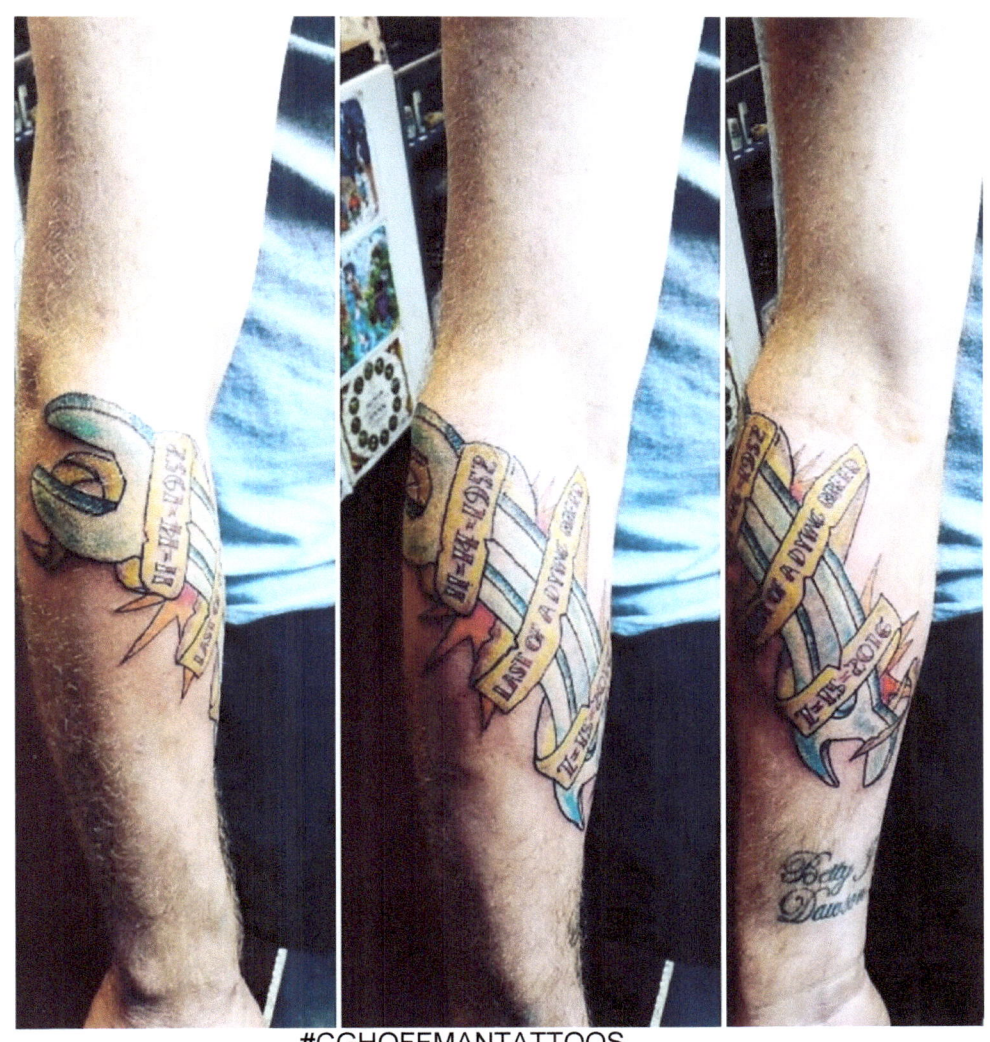

#CGHOFFMANTATTOOS

Custom tattoo by:cghoffman; you don't see your sketch till the day off your apt.

4. Ask For Constant Updates

You found a great artist and you are on track for an excellent tattoo – they are even doing a custom sketch for you so you are pretty pumped…and nervous. Why haven't you seen that sketch yet? When will it be done? What if you don't like it and want to make a few (or twenty) changes? Better keep emailing and calling because artists LOVE that shit.

Reality Check: re-read number 3. the reason many artists will not release a sketch until right before your 1st apt. (or sometimes the day of) is because they have been burned before. Their custom work is what they build their reputation on. If you are lucky enough to book with an artist who will make something unique for you then try to chill and be patient. Even if you only get to see the sketch the day of there will still be time for adjustments. If the "wait and see" style won't work for you then communicate that to your artist so you can work something out ahead of time – or work with someone else.

5. Show Up Late – Or Don't Show Up At All

You have your apt. all set to go but then disaster strikes – your car breaks down, your dog runs away, there is a 10 hour L.A. Law marathon on TV and you are NOT going to make that apt. Well that's kinda embarrassing so... don't call. They will work on someone else...right?

Reality Check: Unless your artist takes walk-ins then NO – they will not be working on someone else. And even if they *do* take walk-ins so what? You made a commitment to be there and you blew it off. Your no-show most likely cost your artist money (which is why many artists require a non-refundable deposit) Of course a *real*emergency means you cancel – but make sure you call as soon as you realize you are not going to make that apt. – the more notice the better. And no-showing for no good reason? The Devil has a special spot in Hell just for you.

6. Bring Your Posse to Your Appointment

Hey if it's good enough for Justin Beiber it's good enough for you, right? So bring a friend or five and make sure you are getting tons of selfies and maybe a little video to throw up on YouTube. It's *your* tattoo time and you NEED to share that shit with the world!

Reality Check: No One wants to be Justin Bieber. Probably Justin Bieber doesn't want to be Justin Bieber anymore. Don't bring a soccer team with you to your appointment. Most shop spaces are small and even if it's not your artist is WORKING. They neither want nor need the distraction (and the other people in the shop don't want that shit either). *If you must* – bring one "wing-man" who can run out for snacks or ibuprofen or soda's what have you. And tell your wing-man to bring a book. Watching someone get tattooed is actually pretty fucking boring.

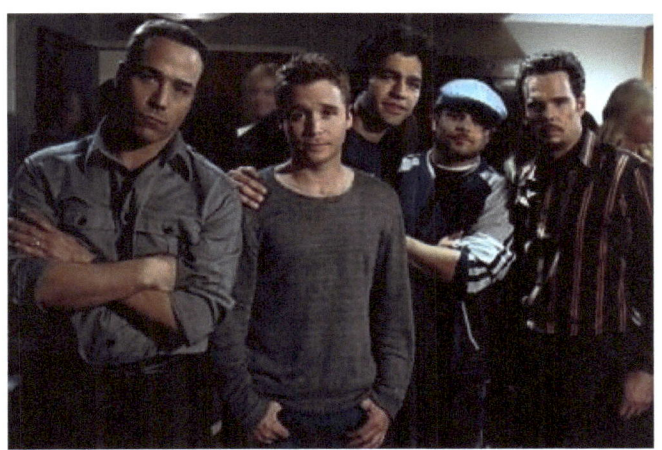
Even Vince wouldn't bring his entourage in for his tattoo...would he?

7. Cry and Whine Like a Big Baby

You are right in the middle of that sweet dream catcher tattoo with feathers and shit all along your rib cage when – *Hot Damn That Hurts!!!* Well you had NO idea it was going to hurt that much! You're going to have to take *at least* an hour to chill before you continue. Or maybe you should call it quits for the day? Your artist scheduled 5 hours for your piece and you have only been there for 90 minutes but so what? You only have to pay for how long you sat.

Reality Check: If you have never been tattooed before then prepare yourself for some pain. Tattoos hurt. How much do they hurt? That depends on your personal pain threshold, where it is being placed, the skill of your artist and if you are physically prepped. Prepped how? Get a good nights rest, drink a shit-ton of water and eat a big meal about an hour before your apt. You can get shaky and dizzy while being inked – it's happened to me – so plan ahead and let your artist know what to expect from you.

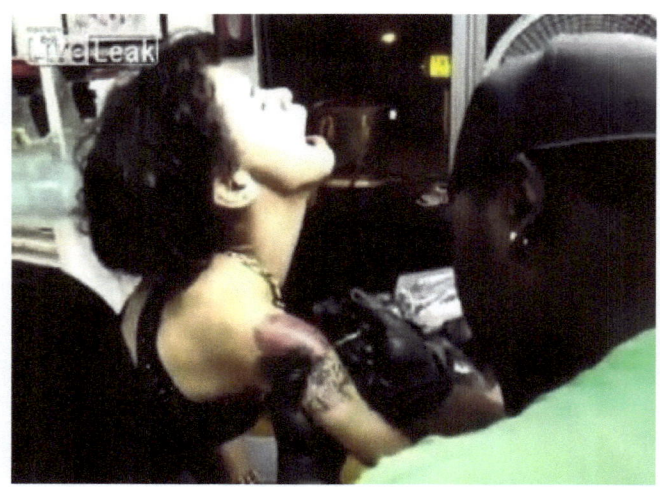
look for the You Tube video

8. Show Up Drunk

So your kinda nervous about getting your armpit tattooed – I get it. That shit hurts for real. Best bet is to go slam like 5 or 6 beers right before hand. With any luck you can sleep through your apt. Win!

Reality Check: Don't drink before your tattoo – oh please don't. You won't be able to sit properly, follow instructions properly, you will get all sweaty and slick and your blood will thin. Plus your artist probably won't work on you anyways if you are drunk – save it for after your session.

9. Lie About Your Age*

Your sixteen but there is No WAY you can wait until you are 18 to get that 'shhhhh' tattoo on your index finger. No. Fucking. Way. No problem – just tell your artist that your mom gave you permission and bust out a signed permission slip – that oughta do it!

Reality Check: Seriously? It doesn't matter if your mother *escorts you to the shop* and gives her permission in person – it's illegal and no artist/shop owner is going to risk their license so you can have a "One Direction" back tattoo. What would a bartender say if your mom brought you into the bar and gave you permission to do shots with her? Same difference.

* **OH SNAP** – I got this one wrong! Depends on the state you live in and the shop's policy. Lots of people are able to bring their 16 year old in or even give

them a permission slip. Check with your shop and RESPECT whatever they tell you their policy is! (and thanks for catching my mistake interwebs – you're the best)

10. Don't Tip Your artist

Whew you did it – you got your next mad-cool tattoo and can't wait to show it off. You tell your artist "thanks bro" and head out to reception to pay up.

Reality Check: Did you get a killer tattoo? Did your artist work hard on your behalf and do a great job? Do they work in the shop but not *own* the shop? You should leave a tip. I know I know – tattoos are expensive, artists make so much money etc. etc. I've heard it all before. Bottom line – tipping your tattoo artist is cool and you want to be cool, right?

www.ingramcontent.com/pod-product-compliance
Lightning Source LLC
Chambersburg PA
CBHW040307220526
45473CB00002B/600